# *Enchanting the Shadowlands*

Copyright © 2015 by Lorna Smithers

ISBN 978-1-326-14190-5

First published in 2015

Some of these poems have been published in *Moon Poets, The Dawntreader, Heroic Fantasy Quarterly* and on 'The Druid Network' and 'Dun Brython' websites.

Cover image: Fairy Lane, Penwortham by Lorna Smithers

Special thanks to my mum and dad and friend Peter Dillon for continuous support. To Trevor Greenfield at Moon Books for my place as a Resident Poet and for publishing my poetry and articles. To Dawn Bauling and Ronnie Goodyer at Indigo Dreams for publishing many of my poems. To members of Preston Poets Society, The Creative Network Writers, The Oak and Feather Grove, The Druid Network, UCLan Pagan Society and The Silver Branch Bardic Network. Again to Peter and to Nicolas Guy Williams, fellow members of performance group Guests of the Earth. Also to Korova Arts Café, the Beautiful Planet Café, The Continental, the Harris Museum and to The Creative Network for providing performance opportunities.

*This book is dedicated to Gwyn ap Nudd
and the spirits of my local landscape*

# Contents

**Prelude**     1
     The Bull of Conflict

**The Dwellers in the Water Country**     4
     The Dwellers in the Water Country
     How our wildness was never at home
     Bone Man
     Whisperer in the Rushes
     Lady of the Oak
     The Region Linuis
     Prayer for Netholme

**Nodens**     16
     Cockersand Abbey
     Catcher in the Mist
     Sea Serpent
     Temple of Nodens 21$^{st}$ C
     Message

**The Green Hill on the Water**     22
     Peneverdant
     St Mary's Well
     The Water Dragon and her Daughters
     Spirit of the Aquifer
     Fairy Procession
     The Fairies of Castle Hill

**Middleforth Green**     37
     The Bird Scarer

    The Blindfolded Spinner
    Penwortham Mill
    Workhouse
    Potato Field
    Wagoner

***The Meadows***                                                             48
    White Mare Waking
    Come Red Robin
    Grasshopper Party
    Litany of the Meadows
    Take Wing My Queen
    Old Beetle
    Slugless
    Dark Horse

***Priest Town***                                                                59
    Soul
    Magdalen Hospital
    Barguest
    Spinner in the Cellar
    Town I do not Know
    Priest Town
    Seeing a Red Admiral before visiting St Walburge's
    Hole in the Sky

***The Ribble and Belisama***                                  73
    Brook Sprite
    Summer Bright
    A Heron
    Ribble Boatman

    Riversway Dockland
    Gulls in November
    Swan over Brockholes Stone Circle
    Proud of Preston

***Gwyn ap Nudd***                                      84
    If I Had To Fight Your Battle
    Gwyn and Gwythyr
    When You Hunt for Souls in the Winter Rain
    Winter King
    The Brown-Eared Hound
    Hounds of Annwn

***Gwyn's Hall***                                           95
    Gwyn's Hall
    A Journeying Song
    In the mist
    Audience
    No Rules
    No Theodicy

***Coda***                                                   104
    Presence

# *Prelude*

**The Bull of Conflict**

*I come from battle and conflict*
*With a shield in my hand;*
*Broken is the helmet*
*By the pushing of spears.*
　'The Dialogue of Gwyddno Garanhir and Gwyn ap Nudd'
*The Black Book of Carmarthen*

On an empty day automata drift,
Wending suit shapes through the mist.
Touchless I fade like a symbol unhitched.
The spoils of war quake in the museum.
Piercing the grey wearing horns of a bull
A white warrior blackened and bloodied
Disguises his limp in an infinite gloom,
On his spear leans, softly says:
"My comrades are slain and yet I live,
*I come from battle and conflict.*"

His dire avowal brings howling winds,
Chill clutch at my shoulders their lament dins
Of hero light fading from mortal skin.
In glass cabinets swords clash savage,
Raging figures thrash on ragged pages
Chanting the desolate past of ravaged war bands.
With war-torn wisdom, sombrely he whispers:
"These gathered memories to you I give.
Gone are the days I crossed this land
*With a shield in my hand.*"

His barrage of sadness barks in my mind
Like hapless hounds on a winter's night.
Fierce their madness, dark their plight,
For the perishing souls they collect,
The past's great spirit protect.
Like thundering wind obligation overwhelms me.
The blade of futility threatens to unfasten me.
"How do I cherish and defend these memories
When like the kingdoms of Rheged and Elmet
*Broken is the helmet?*"

I ask the Bull of Conflict.
His tears run bright with the passing of time,
Chariots wheeling in multihued light,
Victims reflected in star lit skies.
He says: "this shadow land needs enchantment
To banish the blight of despair.
Nurture the memories with magic
And they'll sing a blessed new year.
Do not be pressed into fear
*By the pushing of spears.*"

# *The Dwellers in the Water Country*

**The Dwellers in the Water Country**

They came with the splash of oars
and the steady splash of feet,
drawn by auroch, red deer and destiny,

the dream of a bard
who saw the green hill rising
from a wilderness of carr and marsh.

Moonlit snipe fluted high calls
as they travelled by night,
in perfect tune with the bright darkness,

glistening skin woad painted,
near amphibious
breathing in time with the damp.

To practiced hands and quiet tread
seed headed reeds and tall rushes
soughed and parted.

Fur-clad hunters and huntresses led,
wielding spears or carrying bows,
predatory eyes sharp and alert.

Mothers behind urged children on
as they paused to wonder
at whistling plovers.

Swaying reeds sighed back.

Quick fish and voluminous eels
twitching in dark water filled their trail.

Guided by the river-moon,
lamp of the Lady of Shining Waters,
they reached her tidal pool,

a luminescent ocean, and halted,
blue swirl of their skins lit like ripples,
leaning on barky spears.

Disguised bitterns peered out shyly.
A tufted heron tucking moonlight
into his beard stood witness.

Turning east,
they saw the green hill rising
from untamed scrubland silver glazed,

outlined on its summit a solitary auroch
raising prow horns, uncanny oldness
in his returning gaze.

Knowing the fulfilment of a dream
their halloos ascended,
awakening a covey of barking geese.

Their chorus hung suspended in the air.
To those who can hear, it still remains.
There they built their lake village.

**How our wildness was never at home**

It seemed we were always running,
running after something
or running away.

Our own skins and the skins we wore
were never ours, stolen,
painted, torn,
reeking of tortured animal.

I cannot forget the wolf
we trapped between two rocks.

I cannot forget the boy
who leapt from the ledge into the river.

I cannot forget the fear
of singing arrows nor lust for the hunt
when man and deer are one.

They say this village is our home.

Why do I pace the walkways,
clawing up the boards?

I was more myself when I was running,
clad in borrowed skins.

**Bone Man**

People shun him but spirits come to him,
mighty aurochs swaying in the wind,
a bashful herd of wild horses,
a stag and doe betraying secrets of their family.

He keeps their bones in a timber hut,
sings the spells their skulls
have taught him
through snapping teeth.

Possessions shake his emaciated frame,
matted hair, aeons of dirt
under his fingernails.
No-one knows his age, origin or name.

He roars and howls,
animal by animal travelling song paths.
As the hut bones dance his bones clack
spirit patterns old as the zodiac.

When he collapses in a spasm of exhaustion
on a pile of furs and skins,
wolves descend, shaggy ruffed,
lick him back to health and rekindle his visions.

**Whisperer in the Rushes**

Young maiden cutting rushes with a babe in your arms,
Why so sad? Why these tears on my salt marsh?
Why do you sob as each reed falls down?
Why do you sigh as you gather them?

Whisperer in the rushes, I am sad because my son
Grows older by the day with no father or home.
Our men fell like reeds and our houses burned.
That is why I sigh as I gather them.

Young maiden cutting rushes, in me you'll find calm.
I am old as the reed beds. I'll do your infant no harm.
Make your bed in my rushes, safely lie down
And sleep as the wind roves. Both sleep in my arms.

**Lady of the Oak**

I leave the shelter of my grove, ducking beneath twisted hawthorn branches which weave the entrance closed behind me. Rain hits my face, falling from a heaven of relentless grey. Reading the sky's grimace I wonder what has been seen.

A crow caws his warning. Sprinting up the hollow way I see a young man, legs a blur of blue white checkers and feet a splash of mud and leather. Hair slicked to his head, his eyes flicker with awe and wariness. The first dapples of a beard play across his chin like leafy shadows.

"M-my Lady of the Oak," he stammers, pulling up. His breathless chest heaves beneath a sodden tunic. Looking more closely at my gnarled face his eyes widen in dawning horror. "Bad news travels from up river. A Man of the Oak wishes to speak with you." He runs away in a flurry of muddy feet.

I follow down the hollow way heedless of the downpour weighing my cloak. The damp air already resides deep within my bones. Looking east, rain drenches the green hill, our sacred headland and the greener barrow housing our ancestors.

The torrent's drumming beat strikes bubbles across the marsh. As I walk onto the wooden pad way, the reeds hiss like snakes. Decay bites my throat. The steely cast of the River of Shining Water reflects the glumness of the sky.

In a canoe roped to the jetty my cousin, Drust, sits hunched in his robes. I question what he is doing here, alone.

The river's song answers. Her visions flood my mind. I see the battle at the Ford of Roaring Water. Broken chariots, tribesmen slaughtered, hero light vanishing from their eyes like fleeing stars. An eagle standard flies high, reflected in the crimson river. Seeing the pale flicker of separating souls, I speak a prayer for those doomed to return to a land where they no longer belong.

Sorrow chokes me like bile. I vomit it in anger at Drust, "what are you doing here, when your clan are dead?"

Drust looks up, yet his face remains hidden by his cowl. "I am taking the remnants of our gods and traditions to the island across the sea."

I laugh, a throaty brittle sound like twigs twisting and snapping. "Gods are not like saplings, to be taken away and re-rooted and traditions are not nurtured by foreign soils. It seems the ideas of the invaders have penetrated more deeply than I imagined."

Drust tenses. Drawing my knife from its leather sheath, I lean down and slice the rope tying his canoe to the jetty. The river sluices him west and out to sea.

Wind carries enemy voices. Reflected in falling droplets I see swords and plumed helms. Slipping on the wood and slithering up the hollow way, I reach the grove and ask the hawthorns for passage. Green peace breaks over me as if I'm sinking into moss. Beneath the canopy's protective shadow I believe myself safe until tumult disturbs the trees. Crows caw, anticipating carrion.

Crossing a sea of acorns I approach the grove's mighty king, put my arms around his trunk and press my face to the rough bark. "Brother Oak, let me see into the future."

My heartbeat merges with the pulse of rising sap. My feet become roots reaching downward through mud to the outer edges of the grove. My arms stretch into branches and split into twigs bearing bunches of lobed leaves washed by the rain, flourishing green.

The ground shudders at the march of soldiers, galloping hooves and chariot wheels. Battle cries holler. Bows hum to the crash of metal. Screams and groans rock me. I taste blood and its bitterness fills me.

Earth and water shift as ditches are cut, fields plundered to feed the enemy. Unseen hands clutch my twigs and voices shriek of a barrow torn down and a temple built to a foreign god. I moan at the ache of rot softening my flesh, bowing and creaking as my branches snap and innards hollow. I beg for lightning's release but there is no answer from the clouds of sorrow.

"Brother, let me return," I speak. "The tribe need my support in their defeat."

I step away from the oak as the hawthorns scream and turn to see shredded branches and burst haws at the sandaled feet of a man wearing a plumed helmet, leather breast plate and red woollen tunic. Brandishing a sword stained with blood and sap he accuses me of sacrificing innocents in my grove to divine the future from their death throes.

I smile. The man freezes in horror. I draw my knife and mustering all my oaken might drive it through the leather and slice open his stomach, spilling his guts onto the grass. Attempting to gather them in like rope he drops twitching and groaning to his knees. I read the future of his people and their empire from his pulsing entrails.

Kneeling, I pick up a handful of blood-soaked acorns and address my brother, "do not fear. Whilst tribes and empires rise and fall, the steady strength of oak will conquer all."

**The Region Linuis**

'*Then it was that the magnanimous Arthur, with all the kings and military force of Britain, fought against the Saxons… The second, third, fourth and fifth (battles), were on another river, by the Britons called Duglas, in the region Linuis.*'
  Nennius, History of the Britons.

In the region of endless water
I see blazoned in blue stillness
A raging sky of crimson
And a thousand crashing spears.

The host of Arthur's war band
Reap their slaughter of the Saxons.
In spirals scream the ravens
Round the deep and bloody lake.

Fierce the red maned chargers
Through the blue and flashing sword thrusts.
Quick their dancing footfalls
Through the thick and blood stained mud.

Harsh the clash of iron on iron,
Unheard the shriek of cloven flesh,
Unmarked the final rattling breath
When ravens scream over blood.

Dead the barren battlefield,
Empty the skies of ravens and red,
Silent the stars that shine

In the staring eyes of slaughtered men.

Sad the song of the marching shades
Departing this land to the afterlife.
Still the blue and crimson lake.
Silent the blood stained sky.

**Prayer for Netholme**

I write this prayer for the White One
who loaned to me a mare of mist,
led me across the marsh of time
and granted me the seer's gift.

I write these words for the god
who led me through the rising mists
to find the lost island of Netholme
midst the floating will-o-wisps.

I write these words from Netholme
looking across the rippling mere
to lights of halls and farmhouses
mixed with ghosts and flickering fear.

I write this prayer for Netholme,
forgotten island in the mist,
for the drained off mere, the bulrushes,
bitterns, cranes and fishermen.

I write this prayer for the souls
of the long forgotten dead
who greet us still in the fields,
wandering roads and haunted farmsteads.

I write these words for the guide
of the long forgotten dead
whose stories must be told
for future hope to live.

# *Nodens*

**Cockersand Abbey**

*'To the god Mars Nodontis, the College of Lictors [and]
Lucianus Aprilis the traveller, in fulfillment of a vow.'*
  Romano-British Statuette found on Cockersand Moss, 1718

Chapter house meets silver frieze
of dappled clouds dipped in river.

Beacon white sun lights the margins
of eyes; priors, pilgrims, travellers.

Holiday makers rush to shore.
Seekers of ages dress lost walls.

Broken healers see a liminal sky,
on a statue writ in silver: *Mars Nodontis.*

They gather and sing "will you heal us?
Beside the lapping tides and flashing sky,

Cloud Maker, fix our wounds and make us whole,
return this no-time to a holy day."

**Catcher in the Mist**

He waits in the mist
in the taste
of clouds I cannot roll on my tongue

dense air pressing down on my back brain

looming figure of a hunter-king-fisherman
furs and leathers garnished with seaweed
briny with salt wisdom

infinitely slipping into blur
like the edges of dream going overboard

how I wish I had his silver hand
could hold him in my grip
fasten up the net safely

but I am beholden beside the lighthouse
that never saved a dream

caught in a mist forgetting
the taste of clouds

his lost name unrolling
from my tongue
*Nodens*

**Sea Serpent**

*'The water fountain is referred to locally as the Dolphin Fountain, even though the water feature affixed here for many years from the 19$^{th}$ century was sea serpent in character.'*
  The Dolphin Fountain, Avenham Park, Preston

It came down from long mountains,
unmeshing its skeleton, shedding its scales,
fine droplets of tiny water,
what a glitterer it was!
swaying like a cobra
with blue diamond eyes,
an infatuation of ruff and gill,
pipe-mouth spilling
a vision of words and water
swimming against the backlashes of my eyes,
splashing up an underground sea world ruled by Nodens,
spikes and spines of things like tritons,
zigzagging fish, shoals of dolphins,
stones, shells, in its midst
this great acrobatic tumbler supple tailed,
knowing all the tricks, bubbling up,
a sea serpent coming to call.

## Temple of Nodens 21st C

Dream source comes powering back
over the land in heavy rain,
primal point from which this world emerges

the injured or insane lowered into the abyss,
waves crashing over them
in the sanctity of Nodens' Temple.

In every bed sleepers descend,
dreaming a storm where he teaches them
how to man a coracle, with catching hand fling out a net,

the unflinching trajectory of a steadfast spear
knowledge of the wound that heals them
licked clean by his eager hounds,

the necessity of his lost arts
beneath the dizzying calls of two tawny owls
where culverted rivers roar under tower blocks

and roads strain on concrete scaffolds.
In every bedroom lights are out,
windows closed, shutters down,

behind the sheet rain a land of sleepers
is dreaming a panacea in the not-light
of his twenty-first century sanctum.

## Message

I lie on a patch of snow, truncated,
a cold metal plate in my breast
in place of a heart,
one leg bitten off in savagery,
staring up into an aloof black hole,
here before day glow banished the stars
and a satellite spun for a year and a day then perished
in the lies of jobs and finances,
predictable as the setting sun and its swelling.

I am the future that cannot live
for the wolf who swallowed up my toes
died with them in an icy cave,
my withered heart forgot to beat in a reliquary
and the great white bear will no longer be my surgeon.
So I lie and pray for all I need;
skin, hair, scalp, fingers, dismantling slowly
as photons in the sun
or daily blessings of the moon,
that someone, sometime, will hear my message.

# The Green Hill on the Water

**Peneverdant**

*'King Edward held PENWORTHAM (spelt PENEVERDANT in the original); there are two carucates of land. It paid 10d in the time of King Edward. Now there is a castle. There are two ploughs in the lordship, six burgesses, three riders, eight villagers and four ploughmen. They have four ploughs between them. There is half a fishery. Woodland and hawk's eyries are as before 1066. Its value is now £3.'*
  Domesday Survey of 1086

Fireworks or exploding stars map stories,
a tapestry of bursting constellations,
*two ploughs, four ploughmen*
with *four ploughs between them*
and eight trudging oxen,
heavy hooves turning clods of mud,
carving curved furrows for seed to fall in *two carucates*.
*Three riders* travel the night sky urgently,
grazing horses torn from green fields
sweating a lather, snorting white streams,
hearts beating like anvils. I pray they will not break.
Toiling with hoe, turf cart and spade,
harangued in sackcloth sparkle *eight villagers,*
in yellows, reds and oranges
their unacknowledged wives and daughters,
infants, fools and cripples who made our *lordship.*
A *hawk's* eyes stare from its *eyrie's* dark cage.
Strong talons crack bars like a young bird's ribs.
Swooping beyond my husband's glove and fist,
it levies my heart into broad oak *woodland*s.

A starlit salmon out-swimming *fisheries* upriver
reminds me time moves on. I cannot stay
on this green hill forever,
queen of *a castle* that no longer exists,
awaiting the fiery outline of the escort of the dead.

## St Mary's Well, Twilight

*'For maidens oft at eve repair*
*Believing that a power is there*
*Which them from every harm can save*
*If but their hands its waters lave.'*
    James Flockhart, 'De Mowbray: A Legend of Penwortham'

I should not be walking the pilgrim's way
at dusk, looking over my shoulder
for anyone who might trace my vagrant steps
through the swash and tangle of buttercups.

The setting sun is casting his vast aura
with a majesty I never dreamt him capable of,
enflaming clouds in luminescent orange and red,
purple like mountains behind the trees.

The birds are singing as if it is their last dusk song.
I enlist bold robin, blackbird and little wren…
as if this is the evening of all evenings
and will be their last so better make it their best.

Surrounding flowers: primrose, daisy, violet
close and leave a mist of sweet perfume.
A butterfly departs with her case of colours.
The gold dust of pollen is more real than the village.

I stumble in a haze, weary and confused
but for the reminder of my own hands wringing.
I must make it to the well where spirits of heaven live,

where I will be safe in the arms of our Blessed Lady.

I head into the shady dell where ivy tangles
and wild, ragged weeds flourish beneath a canopy of beech.
Through ferns secret breezes whisper
and darkening light is cushioned with velvet moths.

The crystal spring flows pure, clear, unhindered,
into a sparkling pool of emergent stars.
I lave my hands in the holy waters
and speak a prayer to our Lady of the Well:

*Ave Maria Stella, Star of the Sea, Queen of Heaven*
*will you save me from the vulgar looks and touch of uncouth men.*
*Ave Maria Stella, Star of the Sea, Queen of Heaven*
*will you protect me from the one I love and save me from sin.*

My splash of hands is followed by silence,
huge and aching as the might of this twilight hour
until the owl calls, I see her white face
and a starlit reflection in the broken pool.

## The Water Dragon and her Daughters

At the heart of the green hill lay a water dragon. She awoke at the end of the Ice Age when the land began to thaw. From her giving womb burst a myriad springs, carving gullies where mosses and ferns sprung.

At the hill's foot a thirsty auroch was the first creature to drink from the purest, most powerful spring, which flowed into a natural pool. The rest of the herd followed, then red deer, wild horses and the first hunter-gatherers who built their nearby Lake Village beside the River of Shining Water.

These early people venerated the spring. Listening to its ever-pouring stream, behind it many heard the song of the dragon's daughter. It was rumoured she could be seen by moonlight. She first appeared as a pale woman, but look again and you would see her scales and glimmering tail. To this strange spirit the people attributed the spring's healing powers.

A line of Brythonic women presided over the spring, serving its spirit, meting its cures until their last representative was slaughtered by the Romans. This tradition remained in the memory of the local people. Therefore, when the missionaries arrived they moved quickly in re-dedicating the spring to St Mary. A stone basin was built and a stone cross erected over the new well, inscribed with the Magnificat.

Over the years it became a site of pilgrimage. Strangers travelled from across the country to marvel at its picturesque glade at the hill's foot, overlooked by a canopy of beech, surrounded by ivy and primroses. Although forbidden, the healing rituals continued, evidenced by multicoloured floating ribbons. People immersed themselves in its waters, took their horses in with them. It was finally decided these activities must stop and the well was capped.

Throughout this time the dragon's daughter was ignored; yet she still gave, even though her spring was forced irreverently into a trickling metal pipe. Then something catastrophic happened.

The river was moved southward to make way for the docklands. The sandstone beneath the hill sealing the aquifer was breached. Down below the water dragon experienced an inexplicable pain. Writhing, gasping within the chasm, her womb imploded. Her features shrunk and fell inward, becoming sheer water sucked away through the shattered bedrock. The being of her daughters unravelled with her, shrieking backward into disappearance.

St Mary's well ran dry. Local people were deprived of their cleanest source of water. Prevalent whispers spoke of the bad omen, yet the fault of the developers was not revealed. There was nothing to worry about: piped water would be coming soon, for a hefty fee. The well was buried, out of sight and out of mind.

Yet it remains on old maps and in the memory of the land, which does not forget, in a cold, empty cavern and tunnels where streams ran, but are no more. At the spring's old site or wandering the hill at certain liminal times, you might sense a dragon's heartbeat or hear her final gasp. You may glimpse the ghosts of her daughters, hear their last screams.

**Spirit of the Aquifer**

In eighteen eighty-four
a monolithic feat of engineering
shifts the Ribble's course:
*no water to the springs.*

From the hill's abyssal deep
a rumbling of the bowels,
a vexed aquatic shriek:
*no water to the wells.*

Breached within the chasm
a dragon lies gasping
with a pain she cannot fathom:
*no water to the springs.*

Water table reft
her giving womb unswells,
surging through the clefts:
*no water to the wells.*

Unravelling inside
her serpent magic streams
to join the angry tides:
*no water to the springs.*

Culverted and banked
her serpent powers fail,
leaking dry and cracked:
*no water to the wells.*

The spinning dragon-girl
tumbles from her swing
and slips to the underworld:
*no water to the springs.*

Her spirit will not rise
through the dead and empty tunnels,
disconsolate we cry:
*no water to the wells.*

The hill, no longer healing
stands broken of its spell,
*no water to the springs,*
*no water to the wells.*

**Fairy Procession**

I.
Hear, oh, hear
The passing bell, fear
The midnight toll on the corpse road drear.

Heed our chant,
Avert your glance
From the spectral procession of Fairyland.

For fates are we
Who the spirit paths keep
Between this world and mystery.

II.
Year by year
We carry the bier
Down this avenue long and drenched in tears

With a fairy corpse
Whose withered form
And dew-drenched face you would see as your own

Then mad would be,
Insanely flee
From the terror of death to its untimely sleep.

III.
Hear, oh, hear
The passing bell, fear

The midnight toll on the corpse road drear.

Heed our chant,
Avert your glance
From the spectral procession of Fairyland.

For fates are we
Who the spirit paths keep
Between this world and mystery.

## The Fairies of Castle Hill

When Winter's King ruled over the Ice Age, driving glaciers over the land to carve its new shape with blizzard snows and harsh winds, he and his spirits paused to rest at this hollow hill, which they entered to feast, dance and make merry. Wondering at its illumined caverns and the intricate beauty of its slowly forming water dragon some of them begged to stay.

His task near complete, knowing it would soon be time to retreat to the underworld, Winter's King agreed. He assigned these spirits the role of protecting the hill and its water dragon, told them they must teach its people of the ways between the worlds and take them into its halls upon their death. Every winter they must ensure the path to the underworld remained open for his hunt.

When the hill thawed the spirits mixed with the first trees, a surrounding scrubby tundra of birch replaced with huge bog oaks thick with mosses. The first people to venture into these groves sensed their presence in the unwarranted snap of twigs and warning cries of crows, heard their piping tunes and mournful refrains. However, only certain people could see and communicate with them.

To these Brythonic seers they appeared in many guises. Sometimes they took the face of the woodland clad in bark and leaf. At others they appeared near human, as tall beings of bright, unbearable beauty, or hooded, hunched and withered, crumbling into decay and death. Frequently they took the apparel of ancestors, living friends and relatives.

As promised, they taught the early people to lead their funeral processions along the spirit path, to erect a mound on the summit of the hill and to bury their dead with weapons, coins, flagons and cutlery for use in the afterlife. They were invoked to guide the dead into the hill and in return gifted with spiralling incense, spiced cake and mead.

The Britons only visited the hill on select occasions, for funerals and seasonal rites where the worlds met for feasting and dancing. Most times it was set aside for the spirits and through the coldest months it was abandoned entirely for the passage of the hunt.

These traditions were maintained until the missionaries came. Horrified by the prevailing beliefs they dismantled the burial mound and reburied the bones in the Christian way. In its place a wooden church was erected and dedicated to St Mary, who was to replace the female seers who communed with the underworld. During its consecration solemn chanting and lashings of holy water ensured the 'evil' spirits were kept at bay.

Cut off from the summit and their role in guiding the dead, some spirits retreated into the hill. Others vented their anger in raging winds, storming through the woodlands, felling trees. As the people turned their veneration from the hill to invisible deities of heaven it was subsumed in endless rain, unremitting damp and swirling shadows.

By the time the Normans seized rule and built their motte, castle and priory, Peneverdant 'the green hill on the water' was renowned for being an unpleasant, god-forsaken place. The monks sent from Evesham were as drunk and disreputable as they could get. Of course, they blamed it on the weather. They dared not mention the strange laughter, irresistible lures, dark threats and paralysing fear that gripped them on winter's nights as something cold and fathomless swept by, lifting them from their beds. Once the castle had served its purpose the rulers were swift to depart from the hill, leaving the timber structure to ruin and decay.

Over the years the surrounding landscape was tamed, drained and parcelled out as meadows and pasture. As the village of Penwortham grew, St Mary's Church was rebuilt in stone and its graveyard consecrated. Remembering the devilish spirits and their lust for the souls of the deceased, the priests ensured loud bells were rung to ward them off at every funeral. However, this did not prevent their portents. In the nineteenth century two men saw a procession of black clad fairies in red caps carrying a coffin on Church Avenue. One of the men looked into the coffin, saw his own corpse and died shortly afterward.

Irreparable change came to the 'fairies' when the water dragon disappeared. Unable to fathom how and why the tools of mankind brought about the demise of the giving creature they had loved and served for centuries, some longed to throw themselves down the chasm after her. Others entered an intense state of mourning and remain catatonic to this day. Unrepeatable curses on mankind rang around the empty cavern and echoed throughout Lancashire in the wind and rain.

Eventually, their king arrived. Grave farewells to the water dragon and her daughters were made within and at the sites of the springs. There has been no feasting or dancing in the hill since.

Shortly afterward, the woodland beside Church Avenue was cut down to make way for expensive properties, tarmaced and given over to the motor car. The spirit path ruined, the fairies were forced to move their route from the hill's summit to a dirt trackway at its foot running through Penwortham Wood.

In the healing arms of the Lady of the Wood they settled slowly and came to love the last fragment of their magical landscape. Their whispers encouraged sycamore and ash to bend a natural archway, heavy ivy to climb and hang like chandeliers, dripping mosses to adorn hawthorn and elder. The chorus of blackbird, robin and wren encouraged them to sing. Their procession was seen again and the trackway became known as Fairy Lane.

Looking north to the nearby river they noticed the dark swell of industrial pollution had ceased. In the clear waters salmon and trout re-emerged. Herons and cormorants came to join the flocks of gulls. The birds told them upriver an otter had been seen nursing her cubs in the rushes. In this they recognised the guiding hand of its goddess, Belisama.

However, their sorrows had not ended. Spewing noise and pollution from its twin concrete viaducts as it roared over the river, Penwortham By-pass was built, casting the woodland into unnatural shade. The view of the hill was obscured for good. Restless and embittered, their wrath lingers as rot. Trees fall to the road's vibrations, gravestones topple and dead man's fingers creep from logs. To ward off unwelcome humans they skew their forms into grotesque, malevolent goblins wielding savage spears.

As winter approaches their king appears as Gwyn ap Nudd, a fearsome warrior-huntsman with a blackened face on a dark horse huge as the hill, an infinity of hounds baying behind him. Seeing the precarious state of the hill, its woodland and his spirit path, he perceives its story must be told, before it is too late.

# Middleforth Green

**The Bird Scarer**

*Birdscaring*- painting by Sir George Clausen (1896)

A field of hunger
This windswept feast
Is not for thee
O'er bare tree's bough
Amass the scavengers
Prepare the barrage
You eat or me

*Clap clack clap clack*
Expelled like curses
*Clap clack clap clack*
That crop's our crust
*Clap clack clap clack*
Flap off black scourges
*Clap clack clap clack*
From dawn to dusk

*Clap clack clap crash*
A clash of thunder
Grey pall of desolation shifts
A shining light, a glimpse of wonder
A heavenly gander on god's bright city
Where are you when all is carrion?
Behind those walls' celestial heights
Without a care for what we feed on
Damn to hell your untouchable light

*Clap clack clap clack*
I turn my back
*Clap clack clap clack*
The crows descend
*Clap clack clap clack*
I chase them harder
*Clap clack clap clack*
My warring friends

**The Blindfolded Spinner**

Many years ago in Penwortham three sisters and their mother lived in a cottage on the brow. They were descended from a long line of spinners. Together they spun enough yarn to run a loom and the money they earned kept them fed and clothed.

However, they lived during changing times. Crompton invented the spinning mule, Cartwright built the power loom and Watson erected Penwortham Mill on the edgeland between the township and Walton-le-dale. The family were told that unless they could spin enough yarn to compete with a mule, which was many times their daily output, they would have to give up their cottage crafts and work in the factory.

Realising they could not match up to the machines the mother and the two oldest sisters took jobs as piecers. The youngest sister, determined not to give in, worked day and night. She spun an extraordinary amount of cotton, over ten times as many skeins as the average spinner. She worked until she was bone thin from exhaustion and heavy bags hung under her eyes. Her back became hunched from the rigid position and her lower lip was constantly torn and bleeding from biting off the cotton. And still, she could not spin enough to compete with a mule.

Her mother finally gave her an ultimatum. If she could not earn her keep she was out of the cottage.

That early summer's night the youngest sister collapsed at her spindle and sobbed in despair. As the full moon rose and its bright beam broke through the window she heard the tap of a beak. Looking up she saw the outline of a wren. The little bird had been a friend of her grandmother's and a sound source of advice, so she opened the window. The wren flew in and alighted on her middle sister's spinning wheel.

"Whatever are you doing here at this time?" she asked him.

Eying her tear streaked face and emaciated frame, "I could ask you the same," said the wren.

Unable to hold back her tears, the youngest sister told the wren the whole story.

"Oh dear," said the wren. Glancing at the spinning wheels, "I think you need some help."

"Whoever in the township would want to help a wretched spinner like me, bent-backed and old before my time?"

The wren fluttered over and landed on her shoulder. "Let me tell you a secret," he whispered in her ear. "Your grandmother is still alive."

"What? I saw her buried."

Even more enigmatically, "the dead are not dead. She can help you, if you do as I say. Now, go and get your grandmother's shawl from the trunk beneath your bed, come back, take your seat at the spindle and tie it over your eyes."

"Why?" she asked.

"Your grandmother can only enter rooms where she is not seen."

"But won't you see her?"

"By human eyes," added the wren.

The youngest sister followed his instructions. So well blindfolded all she could see was darkness, "how am I going

41

to spin when I cannot see the yarn, the bobbin or the treadle?" she asked.

"Don't worry about that," said the wren. "Soon you'll see clearly enough."

Hearing the click of the door she jumped. To her great surprise she saw her grandmother walk through it, grey hair tied tight in a bun, back slightly hunched in a worn dress. Sitting down at the middle sister's wheel in silence, she acknowledged her granddaughter's presence with a curt nod, put her foot on the treadle and started to spin.

Just like the old days, the youngest sister thought. Watching her grandmother pursuing her art with speed and skill, she realised not only could she see her own spindle, but the whole room was bathed in a strange pale glow fiercer than moonlight. The ache had gone from her back, and the sting from her lip. She set about her work with renewed resolution.

When dawn arrived, grandmother left and the wren instructed her to remove the blindfold. She found that together they had spun twice as much yarn as on the other nights. Satisfied, she showed the skeins to her mother.

"You will need twice as many again to compete with a mule," said her mother. Yet seeing her improvement she decided to give her another night.

After her mother and sisters had gone to bed, the wren appeared at the window again. The youngest sister let him in and told him the twenty skeins were not enough. This time when she put the blindfold on, not only did her grandmother enter the room, but her great grandmother, too. The girl was very excited as they had only met once. Yet, great grandmother sat in silence at her oldest sister's wheel with that same curt nod and started work.

Together they spun thirty skeins, but it was not quite enough. Her mother granted her a final chance, and on that night her great, great grandmother followed through the door and sat at her mother's wheel. Nodding her greeting she joined their spinning.

Together they spun forty skeins. Her mother was finally satisfied and the youngest sister was guaranteed her place in the house.

She continued to spin all day and through those long nights by light of a moon that never waned, in the company of her grandmothers, until the summer solstice. When the sun reached its zenith she collapsed. The noise woke her sisters. Arriving to see what had happened they removed her blindfold and carried her to her death bed.

As she was about to draw her last breath, "please tell me," requested the middle sister in a voice of admiration and pity, "what was your secret?" She glanced at the blindfold.

The youngest sister shook her head slowly. "I had the help of our grandmothers. The dead are not dead," she said with a fading smile.

It seemed to the sisters that voices of other women whispered around them for a moonlit moment. Then her eyes closed and her final breath rattled from her chest.

Inquisitive, but unconvinced, the remaining sisters returned to the spinning room, but found no evidence the other three wheels had been used since they had abandoned their job to work in the factory.

Their younger sister was buried three days later. I'm not sure where, but the little bird who told me this story assures me she was interred with the blindfold, in a shared grave with her grandmothers.

## Penwortham Mill

You stand there like a mirage, between past
and future, gaping windows filled with shadows.
Your dark cacophony echoes the power
of thirty water horses, steaming at
the engines. Smash of wood and harpists's strum,
strings corded, plucked and distaffs spun. Winged shuttles
flung. Watson's drum drives the decadent dirge
of industry. Deracinated orphans
bend and toil at the tortuous looms.
They lead lives stone deaf and cold as their suppers
'til Sunday brings stiff collars and church parade.
The day the bank breaks, the escapee orphans
are swallowed by forgetting, the factory
passed on. And all the lint in Penwortham
will not plug the wounds of the abandoned young.

You stand there like a coda, vacant labyrinth
to history. An industrial god,
unsealable by band-aids, in the deep
and silent reservoir thirty horse strong.
By demolition trucks your walls might be
broken, windows paned, stark being undone.
Yet your memory will live on, a dark
flat face miming disturbance from the water,
reflection of our past for centuries to come.

**Workhouse**

I.
Picking off nameless black shapes,
tossing naked between rough blankets,
the endless scratching of disembodied hands
keeps me awake.
                    I can only sleep
in the day to the trance of needlework,
when dexterous fingers scoured to the bone
lift jugs of skilly not quite warm enough to drink.

II.
Some days I sit in peace amongst dog graves,
little headstones overgrown with daffodils.

I am listening for the dead wagon,

trapped amongst harmless lunatics,
howling at the moon.

**Potato Field**

Pulling it up
like a mandrake screaming,
looking it in the eye,
giving it a face,
its cold weight
like the stone
in my belly
that never had life,
never had a face.
Wrapping it up
in a handkerchief,
cradling it,
talking to it softly,
my little homunculus
will never have a life
the workhouse can take away.

**Wagoner**

There is a wagoner on the old ridge
Travelling from here to there
With a long stretch of road to traverse
And a fear of not coming home.

Reins slide drenched through his hands.
The swaying rump of his carthorse blurs.
His only light is the burning pipe
Clenched between teeth and an unknown end.

The wagon is empty of barrels
Yet their slosh and creak make rhyme
With hooves and wheels mired to this scene
As he travels a horseshoe of time

Eyes of the past look back at him.
His blinkered cob plods on.
A future unfolds in bright lit windows.
Hesitant cars emerge

To drive with ease down tarmacked streets.
Fireworks burst over amber lights.
With a final throw of ember red
He casts away his pipe.

Hoof-falls fall much quieter
In the memory of mud.
Travelling from here to there
He knows he is not going home.

# *The Meadows*

### White Mare Waking

Green grows white tipped
cow parsleys a head high,
citadels of intrigue
to a wild cavorting eye.

Daisies peek. Curiosity paws.
Garlic's time-bomb shards
expand a quivering nostril.

In green freedom she rolls
turning sun over grass,
cloud over bough,
kicking her heels up.
Spring is here!

Shaking off the old,
treading invisible horse paths
of a lost long maned herd,
her restlessness ripples
through green tips and white flowers.

**Come Red Robin**

Herb Robert, Red Robin,
Pink Geranium,
come as Stinking Bob

with Foxes reek,
Death Come Quickly now,
tendril in on Dove's Feet

with Red Shanks
bold as Dragonsblood,
Bloodwort come

snapping Crane's Bills
in an orbit of Cuckoo's Eyes,
Hooded Felon of the woods.

Come Great Spirit,
Adored Mischief-Maker,
Sacred Flower of Puck.

## Grasshopper Party

I stepped through a puddle one day
and lost a Wellington boot
at a giant green grasshopper party.
They thought it was such a hoot!

I joined their ring with a skip and hop
that barely cleared the grass.
My feet would not dance to their stridulate fiddles
or do a damn thing that I asked.

Yet when I found my other half
we became a peculiar thing,
she was me and me was she
in a bundle of legs and wings.

In my clavicle beat a mighty green heart
and invincible lymph filled my veins,
I found I could fiddle all night long
and leap twenty feet in the rain.

How I danced in the midnight grass
as the orchestra kept gleeful time
in warble and waltz rubbing their legs.
I lost my grasshopper's mind.

Now a giant green grasshopper
sits at my writing desk
and scribbles the tale of her other half
in a sun drenched meadow, at a puddle's edge,

pulling on a Wellington boot
with dreams of home as summer ends
and grasshoppers die one by one,
she's skipping, hopping, stumbling… to bed…

**Litany of the Meadows**

The meadows have been shorn
in a rain of grass heads and sedges
tinted with sorrel, brown-white plantain
and shredded folds of yellow rattle
that never had the chance to seed,
now cut in twain, discarded.

I want to repeat a litany
for every spider, ant and beetle
that lost its home, or legs,
for the dead and empty carapaces,
for the orange tip, cabbage white and fritillary,
for all the bees returning to dried and empty flowers.

Now I know why we no longer
hear the voice of grasshopper or cricket.
There is no place for the froghopper
to leave a gauze of cuckoo spit.
All her nymphs have been
trampled to froth.

I wonder how long
this thoughtlessness can go on
before they rise in strands and stalks,
marching through dream with the hum and buzz of insects
and we finally hear the litany of the meadows
with wonderment and fear.

## Take Wing My Queen

*'We are the bees of the invisible.*
*We wildly collect the honey of the visible,*
*to store in the great golden hive of the invisible.'*
  Rainer Maria Rilke

Let us depart my queen,
sisters kiss farewell to the flowers.
Sink your long tongues
into the obituaries of stamens,
one last taste, forsake the namelessness
of this world ruled by drones.

She who builds creatively
finds no nourishment in nectar grown
on the ramparts of technology,
in the cracks of mechanical arms
snatching endlessly
at the noctilucent hive of the unknown.

Hives empty, baskets heavy,
bearing honey on furred bodies
to a sanctuary of wax and comb,
invisible wisdom to hum
until meadow flowers
recall sweet songs again,

take wing my queen, let us be gone.

**Old Beetle**

Old beetle comes with his walking stick
*click-click*
his mating days are done
*click*
the tables are empty the chairs are gone
*click-click*
nobody sits in the sun
*click*
he packs up his wings in a suitcase
*click-click*
mandibles in a jar
*click*
he's got to go back to the soil
*click-click*
back to where he was born
*click*

**Slugless**

Most people do not like admitting to slugs
oozing in under their back door,
magically slick as solder,
rearing shining intelligent heads,
drivelling a slow glide across lino, up walls,
peering round the handle of a coffee cup,
dropping accidentally into tepid dregs,
entering the fridge to nurse an iceberg lettuce.
But they will admit to their slugs hesitantly
when everyone has gone home
and the silence is too big,
the need too great, the need to tell somebody
about the slugs! How they were seen
at midnight glistening spookily,
antennae raised like little radios,
sliding curiously as water
across work surfaces, on the draining board,
about fear of picking them up, though
they are only cold as the temperature,
of their shivery, mucousy skins,
mainly of treading them between the toes.
Most people will admit to their slugs
when the night is dark and shining
and icy bicycle trails serve as a reminder
of their flaxen bodies heading for doors
or windows. We take strange comfort
in the shared knowing they will be there.
However, one of my friends cannot
admit to any slugs. Instead he treads

the borderline, the perimeter of his garden fence
every night, hoping they will be there.
Not wanting to consider being slugless.
And even I, to whom the slugless confess,
cannot fathom the meaning of sluglessness.

**Dark Horse**

Where are you going horse of my dreams?
I fear I have lost you in the woods.
Untwisting your tail from a nail on a tree
I cord it round my wrist as a symbol of our bond.

Where are you going horse of my dreams?
I fear I have lost you on the moors.
Through purplish heather as the old sun sinks
I follow your penumbra in the distance of my heart.

Where are you going horse of my dreams?
I fear I have lost you to the bog.
Where hoof-prints lead over sphagnum and peat
I splash in your footsteps to the cold brink of nightfall.

Where are you going horse of my dreams?
I fear I have lost you to the dark
Until I see you are standing right in front of me
With your tall, arched neck, water dripping from your bones.

Where will you take me horse of my dreams,
With your handsome smile and skin of slippery moss?
I mount from the foot-worn stone at the threshold of your pool
And we plunge into darkness to the kingdom of our bond.

# *Priest Town*

**Soul**

The otherworld calls in smoke and thunder.
Knowing you are not forgotten,
salamanders of yesteryear
crawl from furnaces where you lay,
their myriad eyes burning red,
knowing you will awake
when the last shards are gone
and you are nothingness.
What will bring back?
Gone but not forgotten,
your fingerprints are still
visible on tabletops and walls.
Your footprints descend to the cellars.
When you do not come back for wine,
who will bring you back?
Those who would walk with you
have already walked these streets and cannot
grope their way through the soot anymore.
The indefinite touch of their fingertips
moves further away like the distance
between us on the outskirts of morning
where by blinking the tower blocks
break their eyes. You are gone but not forgotten
where there is smoke and thunder
from the otherworld, where the furnace
is stoked, the fire lit, where I still pour the wine.

## Magdalen Hospital

*'Of the Magdalen hospital there is, however, a tradition that the church which once occupied the site had sunk beneath the earth, and among the old inhabitants of Preston, there are many who have gone to the Maudlands on Christmas Eve, to listen to the sweet peal of bells...'*
  Preston Chronicle, July 8th 1854

Ringing bells disguise their lives,
buried belfries of rats, crows and rafters,
stratified choirs who would rather sing "church"
than of the 'spittal where a nurse kneels
at a bed's foot counting her rosary
into the madness for strength
to iron out sheets wrinkled with age,
bleach out jaundice, sew linen,
knit flesh, bathe unhealing wounds.

Daily she wonders if they see it in her face,
patches of life flaking away
as she walks amongst them wrapped
in white and bleeding sheets,
catatonic, staring into a bell-sky.
Each night rats gnaw her bones.
Crows consume her flesh. Yet she rises
and carries her hymns into another day
knowing above a world is waiting.

**Barguest**

I.
What is that splashing at the gate?
What is that black and headless thing?

How it howls and shrieks, telling of disaster,
comes to take away a little more of my life.

It has no real shape but what I cast
from its shadow in a torment of rain

when it is neither day nor night.
I would rather be drunk

when it comes for me,
puts its miry feet on my shoulders

and forces me home to unconsciousness.

II.
They say I should listen to its warning.
At this rate I do not have long to live.

The tap room trembles
with my palsied hand on the burnished flagon.

Brass framed paintings and horse brasses blur
in a siege of tobacco smoke.

I raise my drink.

At the bottom of its brown murkiness

lurks a headless shadow
like spilt ink that writhes and twists.

Its barking threat splits my forehead.

III.
The tap room rocks with the laughter
of working men; flat caps, overalls, smiles,

still wearing pride with their uniforms,
bantering about rates of pay,

too young to remember
the dark days of lockouts and plug plot riots.

Never having lost a friend.
Not knowing what we gave for them.

I shouldn't be jealous, but that tragedy
of gunshots keeps coming back to me.

I down the curséd ale and shout for another.

IV.
The innkeeper pushes me out into wet weather,
slams the door, douses the light.

I sway through torrential rain
and puttering streaks of yellow gas lamps.

I know it will be waiting at the gate,
splashing its feet, headless eye watching me.

I start to tremble when all I find is cold emptiness.
No barguest. No sense of direction.

No touch of two paws demanding that I face the darkness.
What if this is the night and there is no companion

to lead me through the gates of death?

**Spinner in the Cellar**

She sings of a love long dead.
She downs the treadle and sings of another
in a voice that aches and creaks
with the turning of her wheel
and a high, lost note that breaks the cellar's air.

"Young man, busy in shop windows
with your tailored suit and tight cravat,
do you feel your heart string tug,
a little choking in your throat,
outside the florist, hear petals whisper?

Will you bring me flowers
with steady footsteps and a gaze sincere?
By the cord of my voice, come,
drawn by my slowly turning wheel
to where I lay out my skeins with love and care.

In my forgotten workshop
I shall tell you a story of flaxen flowers,
how I spun them into linen
and wove them into my tangled hair
by this damp mill town's autumnal air.

How on cold nights my breath turned to mist.
Now I see your breath in my cellar
I just want some company
as I lay out my skeins,
the touch of your hand on my bone-like fingers."

**Town I do not Know**

The town I do not know
is waiting at my back door
in the shadows of two chimneys,
rags of washing in my backyard.

In the town I do not know
stands a figure in an orphanage.
She draws the blinds as I approach,
turns out the light.

Through the shattered window
I catch a glimpse of a lampshade
and sorrow grips my heart.

I fasten her out with my trench coat.
A puckered breath on a cigarette
joins the clouds' silver linings
where I peg out my garments.

I pray for sun to fall on my starched linen
with a little wind, a little thunder,
rain to bleach out the soot.

I will not shut my blinds
in the face of my man and children
who flew like Peter Pan.
I will not close my window.

I pull my memories around me,

like a coat in a circle of smoke.
Old town I do not know you
but will not disown you.

**Priest Town**

Priest Town Priest Town
In aching concrete bound
Sighing liturgies on deaf ears
Your mighty steeples rise
No taller than the hillside.
Tower blocks emptied
Hollow blackened tears

Priest Town Priest Town
Used up mill town
Dereliction speaks in match-stick men
A deadly parasite
Resides within your marrow
Decaying your soul
Your precious relics end

Priest Town Priest Town
City newborn
Struggling spirit smothered in your bed
The creeping tentacles
Of a man-made monster
Wrap you vacuous
And suck your heartbreak dead

Priest Town Priest Town
I sing your death song
Beneath the tarmac lay your spirit down to rest
The city's paradigm
Will be your grave stone

The flashing traffic lights
Will ward your final breath

Yet the traffic lights
Are not forever
Nor the hand that brings your death
Priest Town Priest Town
We'll rise together
Reclaim your pride
And make you sacred city blessed

## Seeing a Red Admiral before visiting St Walburge's

This butterfly was an espionage;
coal-black, amber, whiteness,
the celestial gaps
letting in light
through leaded windows
where painted saints stand in line.

It did not flutter in the tower's centrifuge
where the bell tolls no longer
and the staircase
eternally revolves
into a hole in the sky.

It did not fly up there,
breathlessly gasping for a vantage point
because it contains a cathedral in its arms.

It is the spy who knows all, will tell all
with dotted antennae so fragile
they could pinpoint
a star, a sun
shining
on a tabernacle,

a revelation in wings unfolding

and flying away
before I can grasp
what this stained glass
and its coloured picture-stories mean.

**Hole in the Sky**

Over the moon and down through the hedgerows
we opened a hole in the sky.
All the birds fell.
The man with binoculars
packed up his omen
and tended their sorrowful plight.

Over the moon and down through the hedgerows
we opened a hole in the sky.
All the clouds fell.
The girl ticking boxes
recited their names
as they moistened her cloud-spotter's guide.

Over the moon and down through the hedgerows
we opened a hole in the sky.
All the stars fell.
The man with the telescope
left his observatory
and buried their indomitable light.

With sparklers lit by starlight a parade struck up
over cloud-strewn grounds.
Birds sewn together
weakened and flapped
as they approached the grave
and prayed for a sign.

Over the moon and down through the hedgerows

we opened a hole in the sky.
All the dead fell.
The man with the weapons
gave up his guns
to the cenotaph's hollows and cried.

# The Ribble and Belisama

## Brook Sprite

*Fish House Brook, Penwortham*

Sluice feet treading pebbles,
filmy fingers spreading through stone,
swimming a new stroke, turning
a water wheel hand by hand,

treading stars, holding
the setting sun and new moon rising,
up the volume, push down the accelerator,
beneath your clouds all is drowning.

Rising, casting off bounds
you are not like a shadow walking
or stream sculpted in night air
cloaked in conjured water.

In the cleft of your powerful laughter
the valley is a dark lullaby
summoning me out to the glassy sea
where your heart spring is perfect.

**Summer Bright**

Lady of the summer heat,
Summer Bright, life of this vale,
I walked within your summer dream
when your streams shone bright
from syke to glittering estuary.

I worshipped at your golden streams,
borne like solder from the burning ground.
Amidst the flowers and bumble bees
I downed my honeyed draught
and laughed with the leaping fish.

And the world will never be the same.
They panned for the fish. All the bees
flew away. They fractured
earth's hot core and spilt her ore,
bringing about these dark and final days.

Belisama, Summer Bright,
your name shall be invoked again
on a midsummer's night, beside
a golden stream, yet in this life
your dream may not be seen.

**A Heron**

not appearing as he should,
more like a rag, a bin bag, a piebald pony,
a 'what is that?' on the Ribble train bridge.
By the river Bela I near mistook him for a calf.
He hunches over like a shrouded old man,
tucks himself into a ball of mystery,
tufted beard blowing in the wind,
taking off, stretches out, a grand grey dragon
shooting down the long-drop of sight.
On mudstone flats he catches his eye in nether regions,
reflection coming to life cloaked, feathered,
a shapeshifter balancing on one leg,
narrowing from sight, blinking out
into something else entirely.

**Ribble Boatman**

I am a voice from riverbanks where the city ends in green,
Where water shines and all wishes are fine and starry.
Bring a tear to my riverboat and I will take you on good travels.
Pay me twice and I will bring you back again.

I am old and you may know my distant sons and daughters,
Gulls with grey and white faces smiling on lonely rocks,
Cormorants standing poised, wings raised in a wide salute.
In another life I was a bearded heron constantly shifting shape.

Now I am one of a hundred hundred river spirits,
Whose whirlpools turn and splash the banks at your feet.
Where waters whirled, pleasure boats twirled and my riverboat swum,
You can find me with just one oar and a star in my smile.

## Riversway Dockland

Undine:

As I bathe in the street lights' amber glow
Across the face of my water their features quiver
Profanely unaware of what lies below
A recess of mystery that would make you shiver

Their words play ripples across my depth
They speak not of me but of another place
Where images play upon plasma faces
They do not see beneath the surface

When I awoke in eighteen ninety two
Prince Albert came to ordain my basin
He saw nothing more than his own reflection
And those of the ladies in porcelain fashions

The trawlers trawled, the dredgers dredged
Ship loads of cargo were hauled off and on
Littering my visage with wood pulp and cotton
Beneath the flotsam nobody sees me

They speak of pirates and buccaneers
All I've known is riot at the Ribble Pilot
The reveling Manxman was rudely removed
Now it's too quiet amidst the bobbing pleasure yachts

They speak of ships and privateers
If this dock had not opened in years so late

Before the Dutchman I'd have had the Hind
Prior to Jack Sparrow Sir Francis Drake

If the Golden Hind and its dragon captain
Had sailed resplendent into my dock
Would spirit have moved on the face of the water?
Would he have seen below to the depths of my heart?

For views on the docklands the people gather
To see images floating on a surface so blank
If you looked into my world, your world would shatter
If you stare into the abyss, the abyss stares back*.

*Friedrich Nietzsche

**Gulls in November**

bark at the sun that will not thaw
in spite of their promises to pull the boats
on braided ropes of finest cotton from the dockyard.

Where grey November's ocean leaves
the coast to roar over the world's edge,
what *does* that cold sun want?

A memorial of ships on the horizon?
A conversation with the captain who remembers
their first meeting on starvation's salty brink?

Do the gulls woo that sun with kisses
because it was the one they met each dawn
with a prow slicing through sunlit water

and figurehead bold and bare breasted?
Because its blinding point (from which
they returned hungry and dry lipped,

longing to speak but unable to decipher
the crumbs) backlit their straining cargoes
with mythic significance against an oranging sea?

It is quiet at the dockyard now except for gulls
who share their apostasies with seafarers,
telling of a November day at high tide

when strong beaks remember intricate knots,
the boats are released, they pull them back
to their winter sun and there is silence.

## Swan over Brockholes Stone Circle

*Winter Solstice 2014*

In its unheralded approach we swerved,
caught in the darkness of its eye,
its whiteness was mighty
in slow motion,
everything in the wildness of winter's grey sky.

It was near enough to touch
and all were touched
before it flew toward the pink fallen sun,
ripping a trail of absence we ran after
to where sight cannot go,

returning stunned and somehow wiser
with the image of a great white swan over stones
who knowing the skies came to life
and to Polaris, all the stars, the sun
and moon started singing.

**Proud of Preston**

Belisama:

Proud of Preston heed my entry
Hear the voice of ancient memories
Hearts purloined by Roman sentries
Like a river shining bright.

Proud of Preston born free traders
Made by commerce and hard labour
Merchants gilded artists favoured
Like the Brigantes warred in tribes.

Mechanics shift the scene of battle
Raise the red brick smog industrial
Cording hearts like twisting material
On the wheels of the cotton lords.

Step the Chartists to the engines
Pull the plugs release the tension
The rioters face the sentries
Dye the river dark with blood.

Grey arise the business faceless
Fake fulfillment for the faithless
Mass the market for the tasteless
Selling life for capital.

High in the stone fortress
The sentries hold their rule

Beyond the mall and office
Do you hear a river call?

Proud of Preston I have carved you
In my sweeping spirit formed you
Through your veins floods dazzling water
My Setantii shining bright.

Will you hearken to my entry
Drown false dreams in ancient memories
Will the proud of Preston
Like a shining river rise?

# *Gwyn ap Nudd*

## If I Had To Fight Your Battle

*For Gwyn on Nos Galan Mai*

If I had to fight your battle
could I wake every day
and live with growing trepidation
about the coming of May?

If I had to fight your battle
could I prepare every year,
knowing the inevitability of cycles
still face my rival with honour?

If I had to fight your battle
could I do so wind, rain or shine
or would I flee the harsh rule of these islands
and head for sunnier climes?

If I had to fight your battle
would I do so for woman or man,
stature, sovereignty,
or the broken heart of this land?

If I had to fight your battle
would I do so with sword and spear
or resort to guns and nuclear arms
to blast away this deadlock with my fear?

If I had to fight your battle
could I do so until Judgement Day?
If I lost could I let go,
knowing love will never die?

**Gwyn and Gwythyr**

Hail!
Gwyn and Gwythyr
on Calan Mai
doomed to fight
by Arthur's dihenydd
like two dragons
red and white
immortal sons
of mist and scorcher
circle between
two deathsome plights
eternal summer
and nuclear winter
*the old seasons turn*
nuclear winter
and eternal summer
circle between
two deathsome plights
mist and scorcher's
immortal sons
red and white
like two dragons
by Arthurs' dihenydd
doomed to fight
on Calan Mai
Gwyn and Gwythyr
Hail!

## When You Hunt for Souls in the Winter Rain

*For Gwyn on Nos Galan Gaeaf*

When you hunt for souls in the winter rain
With your snorting horse and hound unleashed
I shall listen in the gaps between towns knowing
Through trembling years you come in many guises.

When you hunt for souls in the winter rain
I shall listen in the gaps between towns knowing
Your face is the night storm of the underworld
And you shall bring terror to end all terror

With your snorting horse and hound unleashed.
Knowing through the years you come in many guises
I shall not only hail you as a warrior or medieval king
On the corpse roads I walk to ancestral graveyards.

When you hunt for souls in the winter rain
I shall listen in the gaps between towns knowing
You shall not only lead the hunt or coffin bearers
To the toll of bells casting your glamour

With your snorting horse and hound unleashed.
Knowing through the years you come in many guises
I shall be wary yet ultimately know you bring peace.
Beneath these catacombs is something beautiful.

**Winter King**

you take me back to what is raw,
glacial plains of horror,
the obnoxious beauty of it all

to beyond the ice age
when millennia ago we met
when the universe drew breath,

when the binding song coalesced.
You came as cold wind
and your inspiration was death.

You are the muse that moves the forest,
the ice that strips the hills,
the hunt that runs without flesh or bone

by the force of its boreal will.
Your voice is the chill that keeps me alive,
the poem that sparkles when all else dies.

When frost rimes my window I cannot forget
you were there at my beginning
and will greet me again at the end.

## The Brown-Eared Hound

*Rivington, October 31$^{st}$ 1917*

  Dorothy tossed in her bed as thunder rolled. She had awoken heart pounding, restless and agitated. This had happened every night since receiving notification her husband had been killed in action. Her sadness was still raw and there remained a part of her that refused to believe he was dead. Apprehension growing, like the gathering storm, she threw off her sheets, paced to the window and threw it open as rain began to pour.

  The baying of hounds rose from the kennels. As lightning flashed she saw the dark outlines of horses on the hill, heads raised, tails high, before they wheeled and galloped out of sight. The scent of fresh rain rose from the grass. Suddenly she craved being outdoors.

  Heedless of what her maid might say, she descended the stairs in her pale nightdress, crossed the hall and flung open the doors. Rain ricocheted off the yard. The smell of drenched petals in hanging baskets mixed with the sweetness of straw in empty looseboxes.

  She heard a scraping of hooves, her husband's black getting up from his bed and putting his fine head over the stable door. Dorothy had been forced to keep him in since the day the letter arrived due to bouts of a near fatal colic. There was a wildness in his eyes she had never seen before. When he whinnied its high pitch sent a chill down her spine. She was shocked to see him throw his chest against the door which groaned, but withstood the barrage.

Shivering, she made her way to the kennels. Muddy water from the hills washed down through the yard over her bare feet. Never had she heard such a commotion from the hounds, even when they were closing in for the kill. When she entered she was assailed by their hot, pungent scent. As they paced and leapt against their cages the mad note in their voices made her tremble.

Get a grip, she told herself. You've never been afraid of horse or hound before.

She could not resist looking at the empty cage, the home of the brown-eared hound. White all over, his only colouring had been the russet tips of his velvet ears. After her husband went to war he had pined away to skin and bone. The day she received the letter, Dorothy had found the cage door open, the brown-eared hound gone.

The howling reached a new crescendo and was met by a familiar bark from the yard. Every hair on Dorothy's neck rose in turn. It seemed her limbs moved of their own volition as she left the kennels and closed the door.

Thunder roared and a flash of lightning lit the yard. She saw the outline of the brown-eared hound and beside him her husband, wearing a peaked cap and khaki uniform. His right hand clutched his left side and he leant on his rifle. His face was pallid and drawn.

Dorothy froze. "Malcolm?" Her heart leapt with fear and elation.

Malcolm stared at her, as if not only through rain and vacant space, but from another world. Eventually his weak smile flickered, "Dorothy."

Tears leapt to Dorothy's eyes. She longed to run to him, embrace him, but… looking at the gaping wound, the surrounding blood, there was no way he could have travelled back from France. Choking, "I don't understand. What happened?"

"I was hit by a shell on the way across no-man's land. I died quickly, unlike many others."

"So the letter was right," Dorothy managed a faint whisper. "There was a traitorous part of me that refused to believe..."

"That part was right," said Malcolm. "The dead do not truly die, but ride on the otherside. The brown-eared hound brought me back. I've come to say my final farewell. Then I must take the black, for the hunt will be here soon."

"How can you take the black, when he's not...?"

Her voice was eclipsed by that unworldy whinny.

The baying of another pack filled the air. The brown-eared hound joined their furore. The clatter of hooves echoed from the road. The black banged his foreleg against the door.

"We must part now until we meet again in the afterlife," said Malcolm. "The hunt is here."

"How?" Dorothy strained her eyes in the darkness. There had been no hunt since the men went to war.

The first thing she saw was the coal-red eyes of the hounds, their pale and shadowy shapes wreathing out of the rain. Her knees went weak and buckled. When the horses and riders came into view her heart seized. Many were hunting horses she had ridden out with, the young men acquaintances sent to war, still in uniform, bearing grisly wounds. They rode with cavalrymen from bygone eras, armoured warriors on thickset war horses and stranger outriders, male and female, clad in primeval furs. The huntsman at their head with his dark face and antlers barely looked human at all.

Time seemed to stop and the blood in Dorothy's veins stilled.

The black broke through the door.

Two of the outriders dismounted to aid Malcolm onto his back. Dorothy noticed many of them rode without a saddle or bridle.

"Farewell for now," said Malcolm. "When your time arrives you can join us. Until then keep the brown-eared hound. He knows the ways of the hunt."

The huntsman blew his horn, a sound that threatened to bring down the looseboxes, to rend the very world apart. Already dizzy and on her knees, Dorothy lost consciousness.

She awoke on the break of dawn, cold and soaked to the skin, with the brown-eared hound licking her face. Stroking his russet-tipped ears she pressed her cheek against his damp white coat.

Malcolm's final words spoke again through her mind.

Dorothy wasn't waiting. Stumbling to her feet she went to the field gate and whistled for her chestnut mare, who came eagerly. Led by the brown-eared hound they galloped away over fields to wilder moors, through lonely valleys and deeper ravines, pausing only to look out from hilltop crags in pursuit of the hunt.

They were never seen again, and whether they found the hunt nobody knows.

**Hounds of Annwn**

Countless moons have passed since your release,
death eaters, strange halves of my soul

whose task is to bring all things
to an end within cruel jaws.

Soul deliverers, sharp toothed,
fleet pawed, howling through skies

o'er weald and moor, in pursuit
of prey no others can touch.

Tearing down the troubled dead
wandering lost between the worlds,

dragging them back through a hill of doors
to the King of Annwn's eternal halls.

On thundering nights I endure your call,
turning my hours to thoughts of home.

As you mass at my bedside burning eyed
I feed my fears to you one by one

in minute deaths, aborted and cold,
and whisper my wishes back to your lord.

Hounds of Annwn, your hunger
rules my chthonian soul.

When my task is complete
will you take me, make me whole?

# *Gwyn's Hall*

**Gwyn's Hall**

Summer here and winter there
My longest day your darkest night
Hoar frost drapes your haunted fortress
Whilst swallows ride my glowing sunlight.

Summer here and winter there
My brightest day your longest night
Whilst blackbirds sing my endless fanfare
Crazy owl streaks across your vaunted midnight.

Winter there and summer here
And I between them like the song
That lies unsung between the years
Between your hall and my brief home.

**A Journeying Song**

*I. Horse and Hound*

She will carry me
down invisible horse paths.

He will lead us
to invisible lands.

She will carry me
beyond the stolen skyline.

He will lead us
to where horizons end.

*II. The Dreaming Land*

The dream is not a dream,
it is the life force of the land.
A living memory,
it is the dawn, it is the damned.

The dream is not a sleep,
it is the wakefulness
of past people and their deeds.
It is mistakes and shining laughter.

*III. The Wisdom of the Gods*

The wisdom of the gods
is wide as it is deep
in spirit, flesh and bone,
starlit sea and moonlit keep.

The secrets of our souls,
old and ever-young,
are written in their halls
amidst the flames and fateful songs.

*IV. The Return*

She will carry me
down invisible horse paths.

He will lead us
to break the news again.

She will carry me
to speak my allotted memories.

He will lead us
to where the journey ends.

**In the mist**

I want to be under your spell,
not walking in limbo.

I feel the need to speak honestly.

I want to be like quartzite,
the shattered glass in sandstone,
the part that makes it gleam.

I want to be clean.

I do not want this head full of tears
nor eyes filled with sand that cannot cry any longer.

I want clear vision
only the mist can bring.

**Audience**

I stand on an icy plain of stars.
The fields of impossibility are wide.

We are far too sane
until shaken by divine laughter,
a hand on the shoulder
turning us away from the world
we have made small,
blue and green.

Your laughter is the greatest purifier,
cold as a comet, falling hard
as midsummer rain.

We must learn to travel again
the mysteries of the zodiac,
meet man and beast
in living flesh,
behold the tall flowers
and colossal stones of mighty mountains.

From my audience within your hall,
gateway to the universe
where all the Zoas
march through my visions
in defiance of time

I must return to a full life
made immeasurable,
break the globe and stop the ticking clocks.

**No Rules**

There are no rules.
Break every boundary.
Jackdaws delight upon the gale.
Buzzards swoop in freefall.

There are no rules.
Break every boundary.
Algae's green-blue will never halt,
nor the spoor clouds of fungi.

There are no rules.
Break every boundary.
Even stone crumbles. Rock falls.
The shadows on cave walls will outlive us.

There are no rules.
Break every boundary.
When the stars do not taste good at night
swallow up the black holes.

When you are truly swallowed
the universe will spit you out saying
break every boundary.
There are no rules.
Only truth and promises
bind us in the boundless infinite.

**No Theodicy**

I.
Gwyn ap Nudd, they say you delight
in the crashing of spears in the underworld.

Gwyn ap Nudd, they say you hold the wrath
of the demons of Annwn within your soul.

Gwyn ap Nudd, they say you stole
the most majestic of maidens to your underground home.

Gwyn ap Nudd, they say you ripped out
Nwython's heart and fed it still beating to his own damn son.

Gwyn ap Nudd, they say you are a fallen god.

II.
Is this rumour and hearsay or does myth hold truth?
Well then you are terrible, yet I fain to judge

for you cast no shame on the troubled souls
you gather together in your golden halls.

Why you wrest the battle dead
from the killing fields and horror of slaughter

and rescue those wandering the limbo-lands
of fear and depression I still have no answer.

I see you surrounded by a cloud of mist

with a hound at your side making plans for the future.

As your visions pass I cannot guess them
but know they are won from the weight of the worlds.

I examine and question the ways of the gods
yet make no excuses for you or my path.

I love my life and adore your mysteries.
This is no theodicy.

# *Coda*

**Presence**

*For the Ancestors of this Land*

You are birch on tundra tossed by the north wind.
You are elk drowned agonised in a shallow pool.
You are auroch, wild horse, antlered stag slain.
You are salmon. You are a seafaring people.
You are Briton, Roman, Saxon, Norse and Norman.
You are legend. Your swords and helmets gleam.
You are farmers, millers, brewers and spinners.
You are reapers and golden barley mown.
You are industry's dark chimneys and smoke wrapped walls.
You are abandoned vale and windswept moor.
You are eternal rain and west wind's roar.
You are pilots when the death hounds call.
You are explosion, desolation, dust.
You are engraved in stone and live on as flowers.
You are a child in the world and the world in a child.
You are time immemorial and every waking hour.
You are presence. You are the stories on our lips.

Lorna Smithers lives in Penwortham, Lancashire. She writes poems for unsung landscapes and myths for unacknowledged gods. She can be found performing in cafes and libraries, enchanted woodlands and on mist-wrapped hills.

Her blog 'From Peneverdant' can be found at http://lornasmithers.wordpress.com/